BODY WORKS™

LUNGS

Shannon Caster

PowerKiDS
press.

New York

For my amazing writing group: David, Jean, Julie, Lindsay, and Lauren

Published in 2010 by The Rosen Publishing Group, Inc.
29 East 21st Street, New York, NY 10010

First Edition

Editor: Joanne Randolph
Book Design: Greg Tucker
Layout Design: Kate Laczynski
Photo Researcher: Jessica Gerweck

Photo Credits: Cover, pp. 5, 10 (inset), 13, 14 (inset), 18 3D Clinic/Getty Images; p. 6 © www.istockphoto. com/Nathan Jones; pp. 9, 17 3D4Medical.com/Getty Images; pp. 9 (inset), 10, 18 (inset) Shutterstock.com; p. 14 Nucleus Medical Art, Inc./Getty Images; p. 21 Dorling Kindersley/Getty Images; p. 21 (inset) Dr. John D. Cunningham/Getty Images.

Library of Congress Cataloging-in-Publication Data

Caster, Shannon.
  Lungs / Shannon Caster. — 1st ed.
     p. cm. — (Body works)
  Includes index.
  ISBN 978-1-4358-9371-9 (library binding) — ISBN 978-1-4358-9830-1 (pbk.) — ISBN 978-1-4358-9831-8 (6-pack)
  1. Lungs—Juvenile literature. 2. Respiration—Juvenile literature. I. Title.
  QP121.C45 2010
  612.2—dc22

                                                2009034090

Manufactured in the United States

CPSIA Compliance Information: Batch #WW10PK: For Further Information contact Rosen Publishing, New York, New York at 1-800-237-9932

Contents

Take a Deep Breath

Place your hand on your chest and take a few deep breaths. You may notice your chest rises when you inhale, or breathe in. Your chest falls when you exhale, or breathe out. This is because air moved in and out of two large, spongy **organs** on the right and left sides of your chest. These organs are your lungs.

The lungs work closely with the heart to bring fresh **oxygen** to your body. They also move **carbon dioxide** waste out of your body. Without a steady supply of fresh oxygen, cells in the body would die.

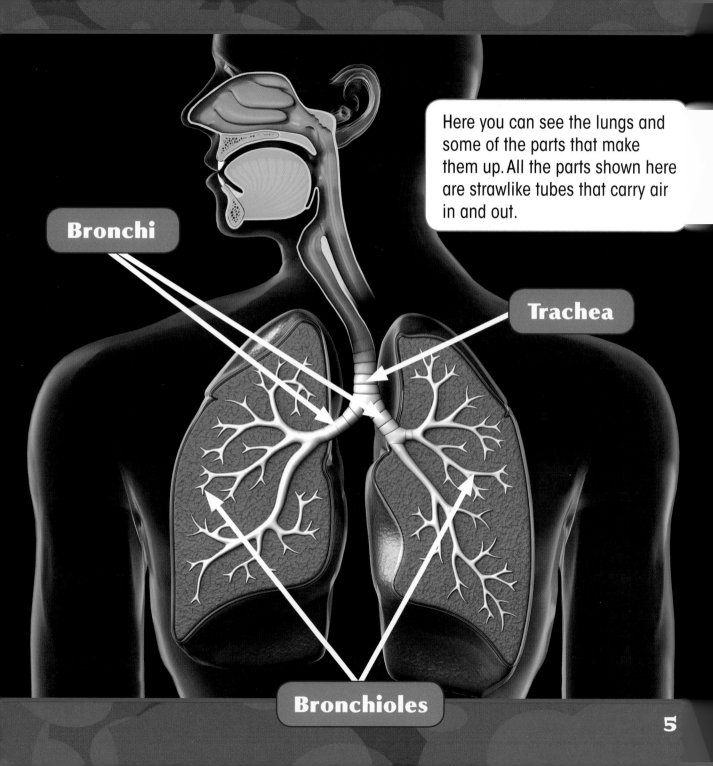

Here you can see the lungs and some of the parts that make them up. All the parts shown here are strawlike tubes that carry air in and out.

Bronchi

Trachea

Bronchioles

Running uses up more energy than walking or sitting, so your body needs more oxygen.

Under Control

The lungs are part of the respiratory system and the autonomic nervous system. The respiratory system controls the exchange of oxygen and carbon dioxide in the body. The autonomic nervous system controls how fast or often you breathe.

When you exercise, your **muscles** need more oxygen. When your body signals it needs more oxygen, the autonomic nervous system widens the **airways** leading into the lungs. It also increases your breathing rate. When you are resting, the autonomic nervous system returns the airways to their normal size. Your breathing rate slows back down, too.

Taking It All In

    Air enters the body through the nose or mouth. When you breathe in through the nose, air moves into an open space, called the nasal cavity. Here the air is warmed and **moistened** before moving through a part called the pharynx to the trachea. The trachea, or windpipe, then carries air to the lungs.

    The trachea also carries the air inhaled through the mouth. In the back of the throat is a specialized flap, or piece, of **cartilage** called the epiglottis. When you swallow food, the epiglottis closes off the trachea. The epiglottis opens when you breathe. This way, air moves from the mouth to the lungs, while food moves to the stomach.

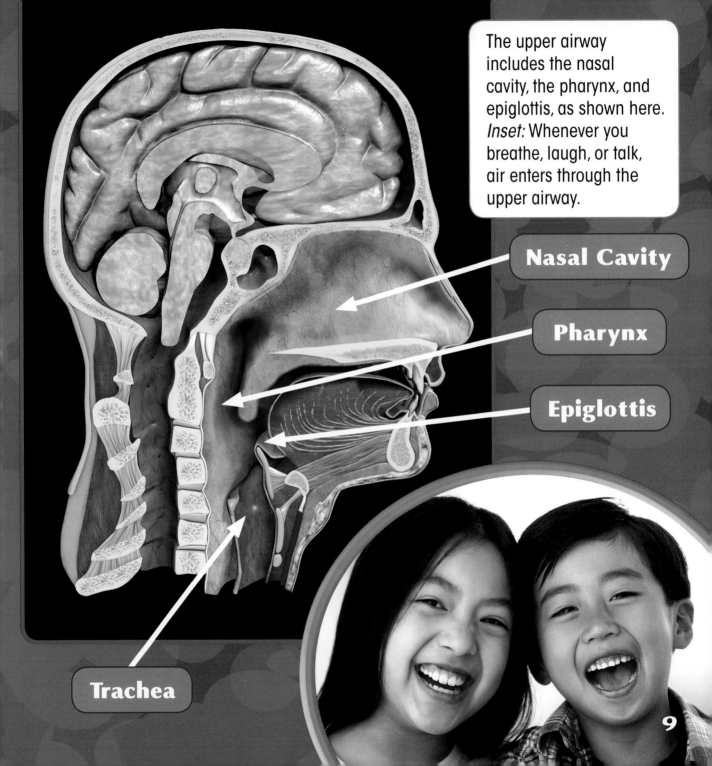

The upper airway includes the nasal cavity, the pharynx, and epiglottis, as shown here. *Inset:* Whenever you breathe, laugh, or talk, air enters through the upper airway.

Nasal Cavity

Pharynx

Epiglottis

Trachea

9

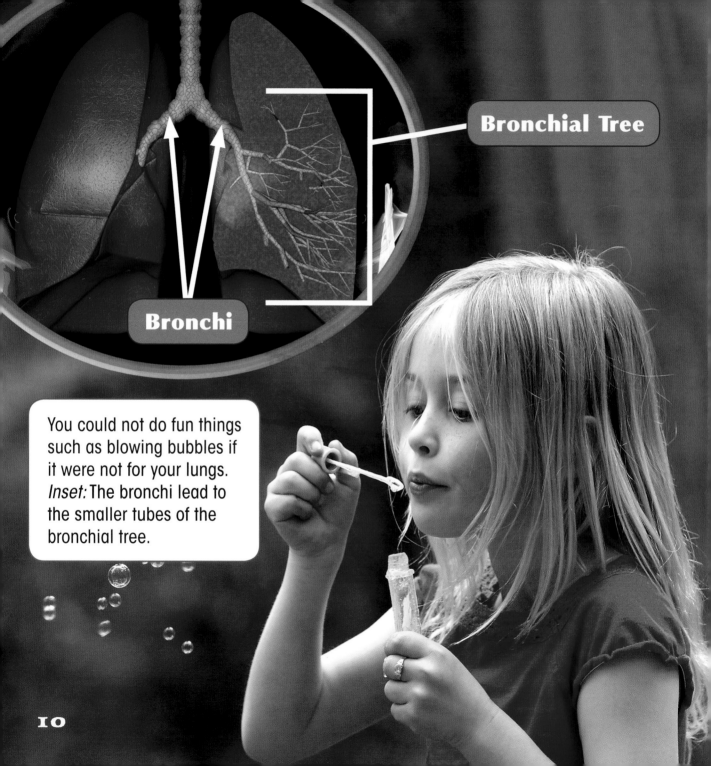

Bronchial Tree

Bronchi

You could not do fun things such as blowing bubbles if it were not for your lungs. *Inset:* The bronchi lead to the smaller tubes of the bronchial tree.

Branches of the Bronchi

As the trachea enters into the chest, it breaks off into two primary branches, called **bronchi**, which are small tubes that carry air to the lungs. One branch goes to the left lung while the other branch goes to the right lung. The trachea and bronchi are made of **fibrous tissue** that has C-shaped rings of cartilage around it. The cartilage helps the trachea and bronchi keep their round shape. The fibrous tissue lets the trachea and bronchi bend and stretch as you breathe and move.

The primary bronchi continue to branch off into smaller bronchi. This system of branching tubes is called the bronchial tree.

More Branches: The Bronchioles

The smallest branches on the bronchial tree are the terminal and respiratory bronchioles. There are about 30,000 terminal bronchioles in each lung. Bronchioles are very small tubes and do not have cartilage rings. To hold their shape, the terminal bronchioles have more muscle in their walls.

Each terminal bronchiole branches out one last time into two or more respiratory bronchioles. Once the air you breathe enters the respiratory bronchioles, oxygen will be separated from the air and then passed to the **bloodstream**.

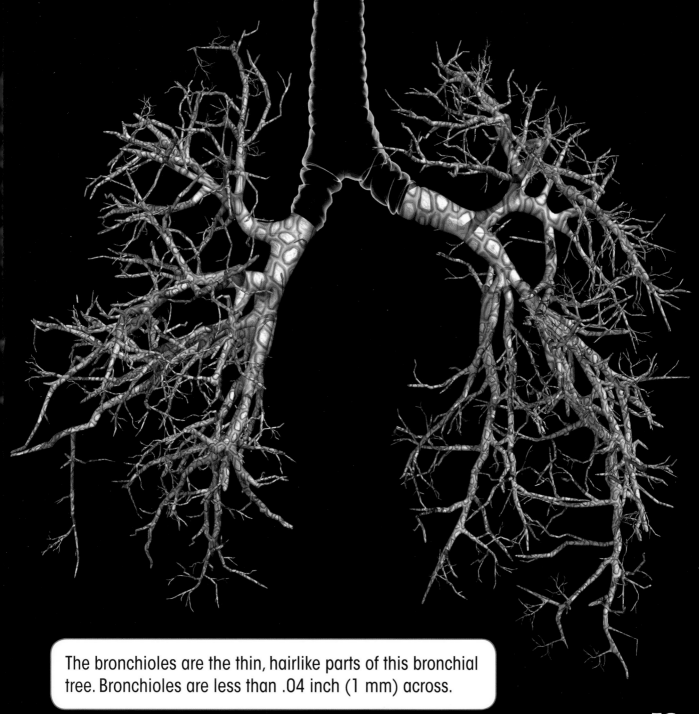

The bronchioles are the thin, hairlike parts of this bronchial tree. Bronchioles are less than .04 inch (1 mm) across.

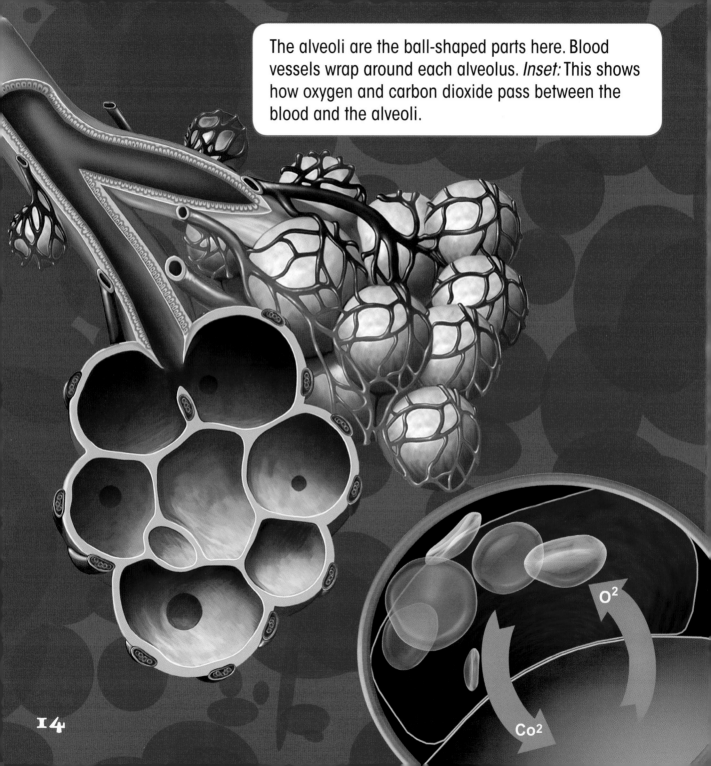

The alveoli are the ball-shaped parts here. Blood vessels wrap around each alveolus. *Inset:* This shows how oxygen and carbon dioxide pass between the blood and the alveoli.

O^2

Co^2

Body Balloons

Tiny balloonlike sacs called alveoli are located at the end of each respiratory bronchiole. When air enters the alveoli, oxygen moves through the thin sac walls into the bloodstream. Carbon dioxide waste moves out of the blood back into the alveoli. The carbon dioxide waste then moves out of the body through the lungs.

Since the walls of the alveoli are so thin, germs, dust, and harmful **chemicals** can easily enter the bloodstream. To keep germs out, the alveoli have **white blood cells** in them. The white blood cells destroy these things so your body will not get sick.

Into the Bloodstream

The lungs need blood from the heart to send fresh oxygen to your body. The pulmonary artery brings blood that has little oxygen to the lungs from the heart.

This oxygen-poor blood moves into tiny blood vessels, called capillaries. Because of their thin walls, the capillaries can pass the carbon dioxide waste to the lungs and pick up fresh oxygen. Once the blood has oxygen, the pulmonary vein carries it from the lungs back to the heart. The heart then pumps this oxygen-rich blood throughout the body.

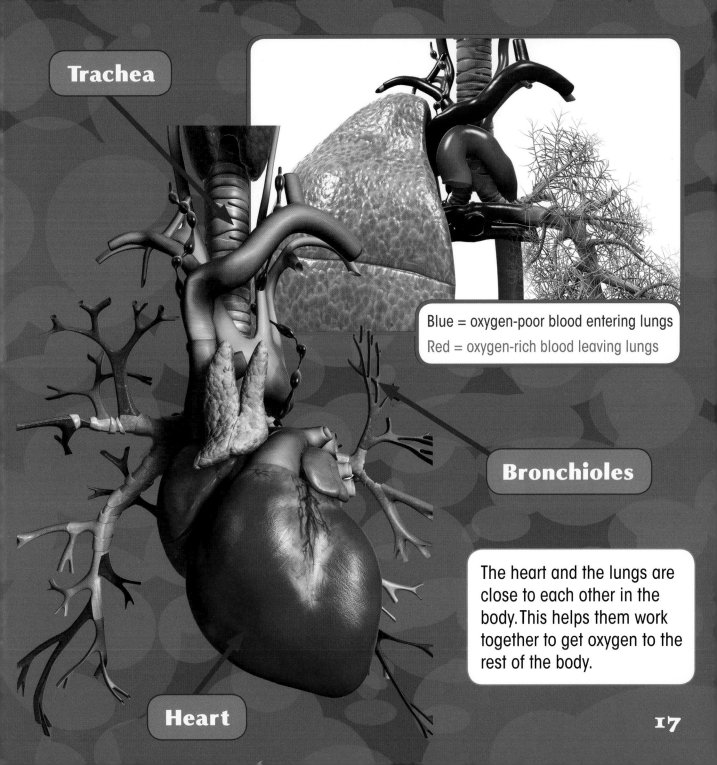

Trachea

Blue = oxygen-poor blood entering lungs
Red = oxygen-rich blood leaving lungs

Bronchioles

The heart and the lungs are close to each other in the body. This helps them work together to get oxygen to the rest of the body.

Heart

17

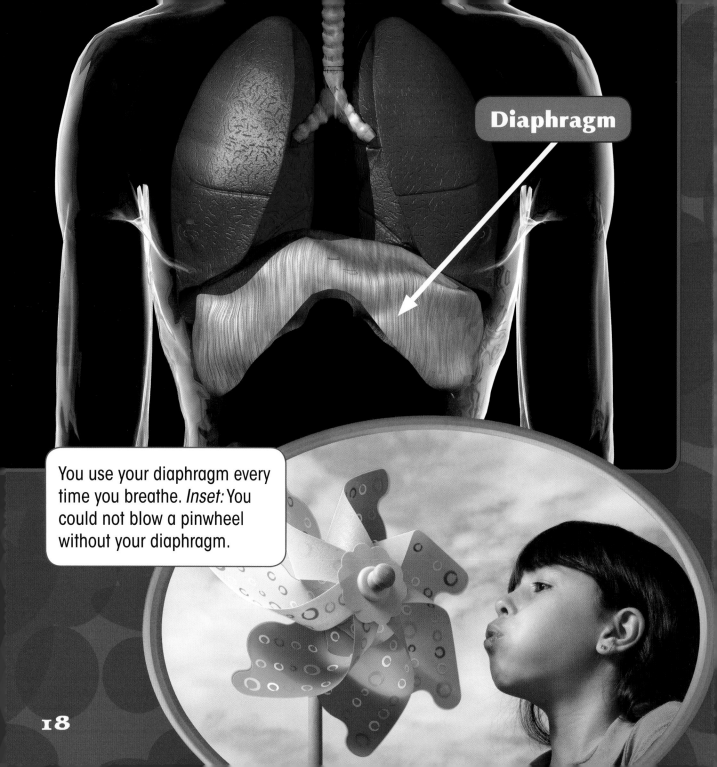

Diaphragm

You use your diaphragm every time you breathe. *Inset:* You could not blow a pinwheel without your diaphragm.

Inhale and Exhale

When you inhale, air rushes into your lungs. In order for your lungs to expand, or grow bigger, to let air in, space must be made inside your chest.

Your diaphragm is a large muscle below your lungs. When you inhale, the diaphragm contracts, or tightens, and flattens out. This pulls the diaphragm down, giving your lungs room to expand. Likewise, muscles between the bones in your **rib cage** also contract when you inhale. This pulls the rib cage up and out. When you exhale, your lungs need less space, so the diaphragm and other muscles relax. This raises your diaphragm upward and pulls your ribs inward.

All Wrapped Up

The lungs need moisture, or wetness, to move freely during breathing. To help the lungs stay moist and healthy, each lung is wrapped in a thin membrane, kind of like a thin skin. This skin is called the pleura, or pleural membrane.

Your chest wall is also lined with a pleural membrane. The pleural membranes keep moisture in and germs that could make you sick out. In between the pleural membranes is a small space filled with fluid, or watery matter. This space allows the membranes to smoothly slide over each other when you breathe in and out.

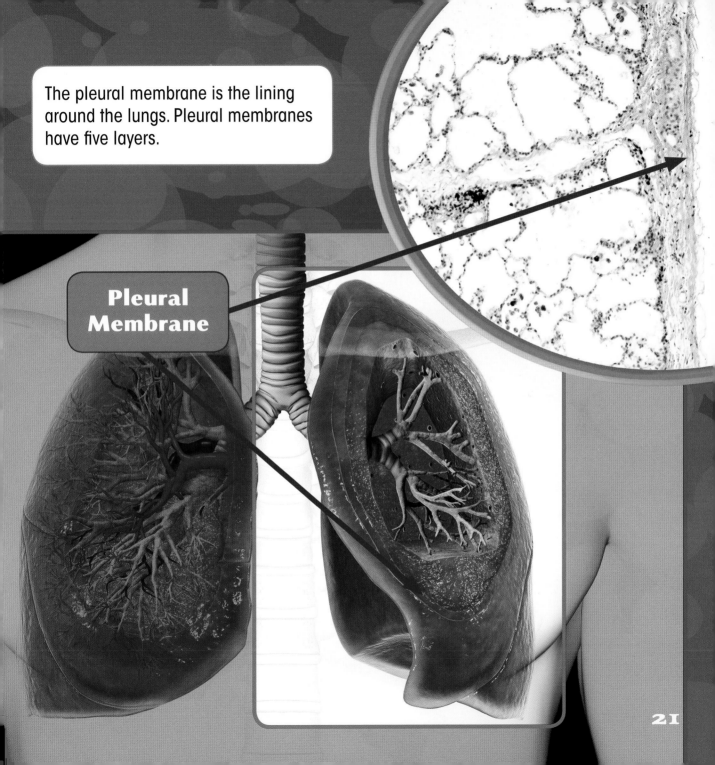

The pleural membrane is the lining around the lungs. Pleural membranes have five layers.

Pleural Membrane

Lung Trouble

Generally we do not think about breathing until something goes wrong. Sometimes people get pneumonia, an illness in which fluid builds up in the airways and keeps the lungs from working the right way. A person with pneumonia might have trouble breathing, chest pain, and a fever. A doctor may give this person medicine, or drugs, to make the illness go away.

Some people have an illness called asthma. Asthma makes the airways smaller, which makes it hard to take a breath. A person with asthma might use an inhaler, which puts medicine into the air for the person to breathe. This medicine opens the airways again.

Glossary

airways (EHR-wayz) Tunnels for air that tie the nose or mouth to the lungs.

bloodstream (BLUD-streem) The flow of blood through the body.

bronchi (BRON-kee) Two tubes in the chest that bring air to each of the lungs.

carbon dioxide (KAR-bin dy-OK-syd) A gas that the body makes to get rid of waste.

cartilage (KAHR-tuh-lij) The bendable matter from which people's nose and ears are made.

chemicals (KEH-mih-kulz) Matter that can be mixed with other matter to cause changes.

fibrous tissue (FY-brus TIH-shoo) Long, strong, threadlike matter in the body.

moistened (MOY-send) Made wet.

muscles (MUH-sulz) Parts of the body that make the body move.

organs (OR-ganz) Parts inside the body that do a job.

oxygen (OK-sih-jen) A gas that has no color, taste, or odor and that people and animals need to breathe.

rib cage (RIB KAYJ) The bones that keep the chest and lungs safe.

white blood cells (WYT BLUD SELZ) Cells that help the body fight illnesses.

Index

Web Sites

Due to the changing nature of Internet links, PowerKids Press has developed an online list of Web sites related to the subject of this book. This site is updated regularly. Please use this link to access the list:
www.powerkidslinks.com/hybw/lung/